EASTER
to
PENTECOST

Year A

Daily Meditations
on the Readings of Easter
to Pentecost

(Reprinted from *Vision 2000*)

Mark Link, S.J.

ThomasMore®
– An RCL Company –
Allen, Texas

IMPRIMI POTEST
Bradley M. Schaeffer, S.J.

NIHIL OBSTAT
Rev. Msgr. Glenn D. Gardner, J.C.D.
Censor Librorum

IMPRIMATUR
† Most Rev. Charles V. Grahmann
Bishop of Dallas

October 9, 1992

The Nihil Obstat and Imprimatur are official declarations
that the material reviewed is free of doctrinal or moral
error. No implication is contained therein that those
granting the Nihil Obstat and Imprimatur agree with the
contents, opinions, or statements expressed.

Cover photo: SuperStock

ACKNOWLEDGMENT
Unless otherwise noted, all Scripture quotations are from
Today's English Version text. Copyright © American
Bible Society 1966, 1971, 1976. Used by permission.

Send all inquiries to:
Thomas More® Publishing
An RCL Company
200 East Bethany Drive
Allen, Texas 75002-3804

Toll Free   800-264-0368
Fax   800-688-8356
Vision 2000 on Internet—htty://v2000.org

Printed in the United States of America

ISBN 0-88347-402-6

1 2 3 4 5   02 01 00 99 98

CONTENTS

How to Use *Easter to Pentecost*

This booklet involves a twofold commitment:

- to meditate daily on your own for ten minutes,
- to meet weekly with six or eight friends for thirty or forty minutes to share your reflections on the daily meditation exercises.

Daily Meditation

Each daily meditation exercise contains four parts:

- a Scripture passage,
- a story,
- an application to life, and
- a concluding thought.

A daily meditation procedure is described on the inside front cover of this book. Begin each daily meditation by praying the following prayer reverently:

Father, you created me
and put me on earth for a purpose.
Jesus, you died for me
and called me to complete your work.
Holy Spirit, you help me
to carry out the work
for which I was created and called.
In your presence and name—
Father, Son, and Holy Spirit—
I begin my meditation.

Weekly Meeting

The purpose of the weekly meeting
is for *support* and *sharing*.
Meetings are 30 to 40 minutes long,
unless the group decides otherwise."

The meeting proper begins
with the leader responding briefly
to these two questions:

- How faithful was I to my commitment
  to reflect daily on the Bible reading?
- Which daily meditation
  was most meaningful for me and why?

The leader then invites each member,
in turn, to respond briefly
to the same two questions.
When all have responded,
the leader opens the floor
to anyone who wishes—

- to elaborate on his or her response
  to the second question or
- to comment on another's response
  (not to take issue with it,
  but to affirm or clarify it).

The meeting ends
with a "call to mission": a charge
to witness to Jesus and
to his teaching in daily life.

The weekly meeting procedure is described
on page 64.

WEEK 1
OF
EASTER

SUNDAY

_____ Easter

*[When John looked into the empty tomb
of Jesus,] he saw and believed.*

JOHN 20:8

A high school student writes:
"I had just finished my paper route
on Easter morning.
As I passed Saint Gall's church,
the sun was coming up.
I didn't intend to go in for Mass,
because I was in the midst
of a teenage rejection of the Church.
Then it happened!
The sun hit the big silver cross
in front of the church.
I couldn't take my eyes off it.
Its fiery brightness made me realize
how the apostles must have felt
on the first Easter. An unseen force
directed my feet up the church steps.
I went in, knelt down, and prayed.
For the first time in my life,
I understood what Easter was all about."
(slightly adapted)

What does Easter mean to me?
What was my most memorable Easter?

*The Gospels do not explain Easter;
Easter explains the Gospels.*

J.S. WHALE (slightly adapted)

MONDAY
Easter
Week 1 _____

[The women left Jesus' tomb] in a hurry,
afraid and yet filled with joy,
and [they] ran to tell his disciples.

MATTHEW 28:8

One of the most convincing proofs
of the resurrection
is the transformation that took place
in Jesus' followers after it.
"Off they went with burning urgency
to tell the news to all the world.
The Messiah had come.
Truly the Kingdom of God was at hand.
Their lives were led for that end,
and for that end alone.
No amount of persecution
could stop them."

B. F. RHEIN

To what extent do I feel an "urgency"
to share the good news of Jesus
with others? With whom, especially?

The lives [of Jesus' followers] . . .
changed the course of human history.
No reasonable explanation
has ever been given
to account for their transformed lives
except their own:
they had seen Jesus alive.

ROBERT L. CLEATH

[Jesus said to Mary Magdalene,]
"Do not hold on to me. . . .
But go to my brothers and tell them
that I am returning to him
who is my Father and their Father,
my God and their God."

JOHN 20:17

A mother had just returned home
from driving her only son to college.
She began to cry,
realizing that his new world
would never be her world—their world.
After the pain of separation wore off,
however, she made a big discovery.
By "letting go" of her son,
she found that she could love him
in a whole new way—
a more fulfilling way, an adult way.
Mary Magdalene
discovered the same thing
after she "let go" of the earthly Jesus
and began to relate to the risen Jesus.

What might I be holding on to
that, perhaps, I should let go of?

That which you cannot let go of,
you do not possess.
It possesses you.

IVERN BALL (slightly adapted)

WEDNESDAY
Easter
Week 1 _____

*[Two brokenhearted disciples, unaware that
Jesus had risen, were returning home
to Emmaus on Easter Sunday morning.
Jesus drew near and walked with them.
He talked to them about the Scriptures,
but they did not recognize him.
When they got to Emmaus,
the two men invited Jesus in to eat.]
He sat down . . . took the bread,
and said the blessing; then he broke
the bread and gave it to them . . .
and they recognized him.*

LUKE 24:30–31

In the resurrection stories the disciples
consistently failed to recognize Jesus
when he appeared to them.
Magdalene thought he was a gardener.
The Emmaus disciples
thought he was a lonely traveler.
The disciples on the seashore
thought he was a beachcomber.

How hard is it for me to recognize
the risen Jesus in our world? Why?

*Three things in the Emmaus story
contributed to the recognition of Jesus:
the broken hearts of the two disciples,
the broken word of the Scriptures,
the broken bread of the Eucharist.*

[Suddenly Jesus appeared
to his disciples in the upper room.]
They were terrified,
thinking that they were seeing a ghost.
But he said to them . . .
"Look at my hands and my feet,
and see that it is I myself. . . ."
They still could not believe,
they were so full of joy and wonder.

LUKE 24:37–39, 41

In his book *But That I Can Believe,*
John A. Robinson describes
how the disciples must have felt
before and after Jesus appeared to them:
"Jesus was someone they had known
and loved and lost. . . . It was all over. . . .
And then it happened. . . .
The life they had known and shared
was not buried with him,
but alive in them.
Jesus was not a dead memory,
but a living presence."

Where and when do I sometimes
experience the living presence of Jesus?

"Where two or three come together
in my name,
I am there with them."

MATTHEW 18:20

FRIDAY
Easter
Week 1 _____

[One of Jesus' Easter appearances
was to disciples on the seashore.
They were in a boat, fishing.
Standing on the beach was Jesus.
The disciples didn't recognize him at first.
Jesus yelled to them to lower their nets.
They did and made a great catch.]
Peter . . . dragged the net ashore
full of big fish,
a hundred and fifty-three in all;
even though there were so many,
still the net did not tear.   JOHN 21:11

The number 153 seems to be significant.
Ancient zoologists said there were
153 different fish in the world.
The number is thought to be symbolic
of all the nations of the world.
Likewise, the net seems to be symbolic,
standing for the Church,
which is destined to embrace
all the nations of the world.

What is one way I might contribute to
the bringing of the good news of Jesus
to all the nations of the world?

[Our job] is not to do something
for the Church,
but to do something *with* it.
                    JOSEPH F. NEWTON

[On another occasion,]
Jesus appeared to the eleven disciples
as they were eating. . . .
He said to them,
"Go throughout the whole world
and preach the gospel to all mankind."

MARK 16:14–15

The capital of Texas is named after
Stephen Austin, an early pioneer,
who founded many settlements in Texas.
Austin didn't like preachers
because they condemned his saloons
and the crime they spawned.
One man who knew Austin well
quoted him as saying that one preacher
could stir up more trouble
than a dozen horse thieves.

The story of Austin reminds us
that Jesus intended his disciples
to stir up trouble–to war against evil.
Jesus said, "I did not come to bring peace,
but a sword" (MATTHEW 10:34).
What is one way
that I could play a more active role
in the war against evil?

No one ever made more trouble
than the "gentle Jesus, meek and mild."

JAMES M. GILLIS

WEEK 2
OF
EASTER

[Thomas was absent
when Jesus appeared to the disciples.
And he refused to believe, saying,]
"Unless I see the scars of the nails
in his hands and put my finger
on those scars and my hand in his side,
I will not believe."
[Later, Jesus reappeared.
This time Thomas was there,
and Jesus said to him,]
"Reach out your hand and put it in my side.
Stop your doubting and believe!"

JOHN 20:25, 27

"Pigeon Feathers" is a story about a boy
who begins to have doubts about Jesus.
One night in bed,
the boy decides upon an experiment.
He lifts his hand above his head and
asks Jesus to touch it. Then he waits.
After a while he puts his hands down again,
not sure if Jesus touched him or not.

We all crave assurance of our faith.
In the end, however, faith is saying
to Jesus, "I trust you!"
Why do I find it hard to trust Jesus?

Sorrow looks back,
worry looks around, faith looks up.
ANONYMOUS

MONDAY
Easter
Week 2 _____

[Jesus said to Nicodemus,]
"No one can enter the Kingdom of God
unless he is born of water and the Spirit.
A person is born physically
of human parents,
but he is born spiritually of the Spirit."

JOHN 3:5–6

George Foreman,
former heavyweight boxing champion,
had been attending Bible classes
and was in a prayer group.
But he seemed to have no spiritual life.
One night after a fight,
he sat in the dressing room
with his head in his hands.
Suddenly he noticed blood
from a cut in his head,
dripping through his hands
onto his bare feet. Then it hit him.
These were the bloody wounds of Jesus:
head, feet, and hands.
That unusual thought was the start
of a spiritual rebirth for him.

What was an especially memorable moment
in my own spiritual life?

The person
who isn't busy being born is busy dying.

BOB DYLAN (slightly adapted)

[Jesus said about the Holy Spirit,]
"The wind blows wherever it wishes;
you hear the sound it makes,
but you do not know
where it comes from or where it is going."
JOHN 3:8

A town drunk underwent a conversion.
An old crony ridiculed him, saying,
"Surely you don't believe all that stuff
about Jesus turning water into wine?"
The ex-drunk said, "I don't know
if Jesus did that or not, but I do know
that he turned wine into food
in my house."
This fits Jesus' point when he says
that we can't see the wind,
but we can hear the sound it makes.
In other words, we can't understand
the Holy Spirit, but we can understand
the Spirit's impact on our lives.

How has the Spirit affected my life—
or the life of someone I know about?

"I will lead my blind people
by roads they have never traveled.
I will turn their darkness into light. . . .
These are my promises,
and I will keep them without fail."
ISAIAH 42:16

WEDNESDAY
Easter
Week 2 _____

God loved the world so much
that he gave his only Son,
so that everyone who believes in him
may not die but have eternal life.

JOHN 3:16

When a friend asked 80-year-old
John Quincy Adams how he was,
he replied, "John is very well, thank you.
But the house he lives in
is sadly dilapidated.
It is tottering on its foundations.
The walls are badly shattered
and the roof is worn.
The building trembles with every wind,
and I think John Quincy Adams
will have to move out of it before long.
But he himself is very well, thank you."

To what degree is my faith
as strong as John Quincy Adam's faith?
How might I make it stronger?

We know
that when this tent we live in–
our body here on earth–is torn down,
God will have
a house in heaven for us to live in,
a home he himself has made,
which will last forever.

2 CORINTHIANS 5:1

*Whoever believes in the Son
has eternal life;
whoever disobeys the Son
will not have life.*

JOHN 3:36

Mike Moran was a Navy helicopter pilot.
One day, while explaining his "chopper"
to his parents, he said,
"As complex as those machines are,
their whirling rotors are held in place
by one simple hexagonal nut."
Then turning to his mother, he said,
"Guess what that nut is called, Mom?"
She shrugged. He smiled and said,
"It's called a 'Jesus Nut.'"

To what extent
does Jesus hold my life together?
What is one area of my life
that is still not under his control?
What is one step that I might take
to begin to let Jesus take control
of this area of my life?

*To the preacher who kept saying,
"We must put God in our lives,"
the Master said,
"God is already there.
Our business is to recognize this."*

ANTHONY DE MELLO, S.J.

FRIDAY
Easter
Week 2 _____

[A large crowd was listening to Jesus.
The hour was late, and they were hungry.
A boy gave Jesus the bread and fish
that he had been saving to eat.]
Jesus took the bread, gave thanks to God,
and distributed it to the people. . . .
He did the same with the fish,
and they all had as much as they wanted.
                                                    JOHN 6:11

At a youth rally in Scotland,
Pope John Paul II challenged
the young people to do what the boy did.
The pope invited them to offer Jesus
their lives and talents (bread and fish).
He said, "You feel conscious
of your inadequacy. . . .
But what I say to you is this:
place your lives in the hands of Jesus.
He will accept you and bless you . . .
beyond your greatest expectations."

How trustingly am I ready to place
my life and my talents (bread and fish)
in Jesus' hands?

Blessed are they
who place themselves in the hands
of Jesus.
He will place himself in their hands.
                                                    ANONYMOUS

[The disciples were crossing the lake
at night when a storm blew up.
Jesus came to them across the water.
They were utterly terrified.]
"Don't be afraid," Jesus told them,
"it is I!"

JOHN 6:20

A poem describes a person in a dream,
walking along a beach with the Lord.
Suddenly, events from the person's life
flash across the sky.
Looking back at the footprints in the sand,
the person sees that during happy times
two sets of footprints appear on the sand.
But during sad times, only one set appears.
The person says to the Lord,
"I don't understand why, in times
when I need you most, you would leave."
The Lord said, "I would never leave you
during your times of trial and suffering.
When you see only one set of footprints,
it was then that I carried you."

When in my life has the Lord carried me?

Who never ate bread in sorrow,
Who never spent the darksome hours
Weeping and watching for the morrow
He knows you not, you heavenly Powers.
JOHANN WOLFGANG VON GOETHE

WEEK 3
OF
EASTER

[Two totally discouraged disciples
were returning home to Emmaus on Easter.
They were unaware that Jesus had risen.
Suddenly Jesus came alongside them,
but they didn't recognize him.
They figured he was just a stranger
who wanted company. When they got to Emmaus,
they asked him in for supper.]
He sat down to eat with them,
took the bread, and said the blessing;
then he broke the bread and gave it to them.
Then their eyes were opened
and they recognized him.

LUKE 24:30–31

Noreen Towers was working among the poor
with no evident success.
One night she went to bed very discouraged.
The next morning, shortly after waking,
Jesus seemed to speak to her, saying,
"Can you not trust my plan for you?"
That split-second experience
changed her from a defeated person
into a person with unshakable faith.

What did I learn
from a discouraging moment in my life?

How else but through a broken heart
May the Lord Christ enter in?

OSCAR WILDE

MONDAY
Easter
Week 3 _____

[Jesus said,]
"Do not work for food that spoils;
instead, work for the food
that lasts for eternal life."
                              JOHN 6:27

Boxer Jack Dempsey went to bed
around 2 A.M. the night he won
the world's heavyweight championship.
An hour later, he woke with a start.
He had just dreamt that he had lost
his newly won championship.
Unable to get back to sleep,
he went out and bought some newspapers
to see what they said about the fight.
"Reading through the accounts,"
he said later, "I began to realize
that success didn't taste
the way I thought it would. . . .
I was left with a curious feeling
of emptiness."

Dempsey's experience invites me to ask:
Do I ever experience "a curious feeling
of emptiness" about my life?

[Jesus warned,]
"This is how it is with those
who pile up riches for themselves
but are not rich in God's sight."
                              LUKE 12:21

"I am the bread of life," Jesus [said.]
"He who comes to me will never be hungry."
JOHN 6:35

In the 1800s an immigrant family
spent almost all its money
for boat tickets to the United States.
To save the little money they had left,
they remained in their cabin and ate
hard bread and water, rather than go
to the ship's dining room
with its more expensive food.
When they docked in New York,
they learned the ship's meals were free.
They were included in the ticket price.

Many people
voyage through life in a similar way.
They starve "spiritually,"
rather than eat the "bread of life,"
free at every Lord's Supper.
What is my experience of the Lord's Supper
at this juncture in my life?
What might I do to deepen and enrich
that experience?

The effect of our sharing
in the body and blood of Christ
is to change us
into what we receive.
POPE SAINT LEO THE GREAT

WEDNESDAY
Easter
Week 3 _____

*[Jesus said,] "What my Father wants
is that all who see the Son and believe
in him should have eternal life."*
                                    JOHN 6:40

More than any other scientist,
Wernher von Braun was responsible
for putting America on the moon.
Before he died, he gave this testimony
concerning life after death:
"I think science has a real surprise
for the skeptics. . . . Nothing in nature,
not even the tiniest particle,
can disappear without a trace.
Nature does not know extinction.
All it knows is transformation. . . .
Everything science has taught me–
and continues to teach me–
strengthens my belief in the continuity
of our spiritual existence after death."

Why don't I live more in accord
with my belief that this life is only
the launching pad for eternal life?

*If I find in myself a desire
that no experience in this world
can satisfy,
the most probable explanation is
that I was made for another world.*
                                    C. S. LEWIS

[Jesus said,] "He who is from God
is the only one who has seen the Father."
JOHN 6:46

A college girl said in a discussion,
"I cannot believe in God any longer."
Her professor replied,
"Maybe I should congratulate you."
"What do you mean?" she asked.
Her professor replied,
"Perhaps the idea of God that you reject
should be rejected."
The professor's point is important.
Often the "god" that people reject
is not the true God,
but an erroneous notion of God
that exists only in their minds.

The clearest image of God
is to be found in Jesus, who said,
"Whoever has seen me
has seen the Father" (JOHN 14:9).
What is there about Jesus
that speaks to me most eloquently
about the Father?

As the print of the seal on wax
is the express image of the seal itself,
so Christ is the express image—
the perfect representation of God.
SAINT AMBROSE

FRIDAY
Easter
Week 3 _____

[Jesus said,] "If you do not eat the flesh
of the Son of Man and drink his blood,
you will not have life in yourselves.
Whoever eats my flesh and drinks my blood
has eternal life."

JOHN 6:53–54

Advertising executive Emilie Griffin
was brought up a Christian Scientist.
But when she reached adulthood,
she experienced a faith struggle.
It is described in her book *Turning*.
A major focus of her struggle
was Jesus' statement
that his body and his blood
were real food and real drink–
a statement that infuriated his enemies
and caused many disciples to leave him
(JOHN 6:32, 66). Eventually, Emilie's faith
in Jesus' "real presence" in the Eucharist
led her to embrace the Church.

Emilie's faith in the Eucharist
invites me to inventory my own faith in
and devotion to the Eucharist.

INVITATION
Jesus of Nazareth
requests the honor of your presence
at a meal to be given in his honor.
ANONYMOUS

[After Jesus said he would give
his body as food and his blood as drink,
many of his followers left him.]
So he asked the twelve disciples,
"And you—would you also like to leave?"
Simon Peter answered him,
"Lord, to whom would we go?
You have the words that give eternal life.
And now we believe and know
that you are the Holy One
who has come from God."

JOHN 6:67–69

At a Fellowship of Christian Athletes
breakfast in New Orleans,
sportscaster Gary Bender suggested
five things that Jesus might say
to you or me if he appeared to us today:
1. I love you;
2. I know you;
3. I understand you;
4. I forgive you.
5. Do you know me?

Bender's words invite me to ask:
How well do I know Jesus?
How might I get to know him better?

To be ignorant of the Scriptures
is to be ignorant of Christ.

SAINT JEROME

WEEK 4
OF
EASTER

*[Jesus said,] "I have come
in order that you might have life—
life in all its fullness."*

JOHN 10:10

A woman was diagnosed
as being terminally ill.
For a while, she continued to live
pretty much as she always did.
Then, one day, she said to herself,
"What am I doing?
What am I building a bank account for?
What am I living this way for?"
Then she decided to begin living
as her heart dictated.
That woman lived 15 more months.
Before she died,
she confided to a friend,
"The last 15 months of my life
were the richest of my entire life."

The woman's experience invites me to ask:
What was one of the richest periods
of my entire life?

*I shall pass through this world but once.
Any good that I can do, or any kindness
that I can show to any human being,
let me do it now and not defer it.
For I shall not pass this way again.*

Attributed to STEPHEN GRELLET (adapted)

MONDAY
Easter
Week 4 _____

[Jesus said,] "I am the good shepherd.
As the Father knows me . . .
in the same way
I know my sheep and they know me.
And I am willing to die for them."
                                    JOHN 10:14–15

A young shepherd
was grazing his flock near Mount Tabor.
Suddenly three Bedouin outlaws appeared.
The shepherd knew the danger he was in,
but he stood his ground
and fought to keep his flock.
The episode ended with the shepherd
being knifed to death
as he attempted to protect his flock.
Jesus had an image like this in mind
when he said, "I am the good shepherd. . . .
And I am willing to die for [the sheep]"
(JOHN 10:14–15).

The story of the young shepherd
invites me to ask:
What is one heroic thing
I was called upon to do in my life?
What motivated me to do it?
How do I look back upon it now?

Plunge into the deep without fear,
with the gladness of April in your heart.
                            RABINDRANATH TAGORE

[Jesus said,]
"My sheep listen to my voice;
I know them, and they follow me . . .
and they shall never die."

JOHN 10:27—28

In World War II, Flying Fortresses
flew from the United States
to the island of Saipan in the Pacific.
Each plane was met by a little Jeep
with a sign reading: "Follow Me!"
The Jeep then led the giant plane
to its assigned parking spot
on the island's airstrip.
A young pilot said of the Jeep:
"I'm not very religious,
but that little Jeep, with its quaint sign,
always reminds me of Jesus.
He was a little, scrawny peasant,
but the giant men and women of our time
would be lost without his direction."

What is one thing that keeps me
from following Jesus more closely than I do?
What might Jesus say to me about it?

The living Christ still has two hands,
one to point the way,
and the other held out
to help us along the way.

T. W. MASON

WEDNESDAY
Easter
Week 4 _____

[Jesus said,] "Whoever rejects me
and does not accept my message
has one who will judge him.
The words I have spoken
will be his judge on the last day!"

JOHN 12:48

W. C. Fields was a great film comedian.
A story—probably apocryphal—
says that near the end of his life
he spent a lot of time
reading the Bible.
Someone asked him about this,
and Fields replied, "I'm looking
for any loopholes I can find."
The implication was that Fields knew
that he had not lived his life
in full accord with Jesus' teaching.
Now he was looking for a way
to excuse himself for this failure
when he appeared before God.

If I died and appeared before God tonight,
what excuse would I give
for not having lived in fuller accord
with Jesus' teaching?

If Christ were standing
before me now, what would I feel,
not about him, but about myself?

SAINT AUGUSTINE (slightly adapted)

*[At the Last Supper, Jesus prayed
to his Father for his disciples, saying,]
"I sent them into the world,
just as you sent me"* (JOHN 17:18).
*[Jesus assured his disciples,]
"Whoever receives anyone I send
receives me also;
and whoever receives me
receives him who sent me."*

JOHN 13:20

A college girl told a friend,
"I believe in God,
and I believe Jesus is God's Son,
but I don't believe in the Church."
Her friend said, "But that's impossible!
You can't separate Jesus and the Church.
They are one—
just as Jesus and the Father are one.
The Holy Spirit came on Pentecost
and formed Jesus and his disciples
into a single body, the Church."
(EPHESIANS 1:23)

To what extent do I tend to separate
Jesus from his Church? Why?

*You cannot have God for your Father,
if you don't have the Church
for your mother.*

SAINT AUGUSTINE

FRIDAY
Easter
Week 4 _____

[Shortly before returning to his Father,
Jesus said to his disciples,]
"I am going to prepare a place for you.
I would not tell you this
if it were not so. And after I go
and prepare a place for you,
I will come back and take you to myself,
so that you will be where I am."
                                              JOHN 14:2–3

John Peterson
wrote a hymn about heaven.
A portion of its lyrics read:
"Over the sunset mountains,
Heaven awaits for me;
Over the sunset mountains,
Jesus my Savior I'll see."
A music critic told Peterson,
"Skip the notion of being with Jesus
and spend more time
describing the joy of heaven."
Of course, Peterson refused,
because the essence of heaven's joy
is standing face-to-face with Jesus.

How comfortable am I with the thought
of standing face-to-face with Jesus?

The goal of religion is not to get us
into heaven–but to get heaven into us.
                                              ANONYMOUS

[Jesus said,] "For a long time
I have been with you all;
yet you do not know me, Philip?
Whoever has seen me
has seen the Father."

JOHN 14:9

A lady asked, "How can Christians claim
to have a special knowledge of God?"
The answer, of course,
depends upon who you say Jesus is.
No bonafide religious leader
ever claimed what Jesus claimed.
Buddha rejected veneration.
Muhammad admitted being a sinner.
Jesus is the only religious leader who
dared to say, "Whoever has seen me
has seen the Father."
If Jesus is who he claimed to be,
then Christians can rightly claim
a special knowledge of God.

Thomas Carlyle said that if Jesus
came today, people wouldn't crucify him.
They'd invite him to dinner, hear what
he had to say, and make fun of it.
To what extent do I agree with Carlyle?

What am I to do with Jesus?
I have to do something with him.
I cannot ignore him.

WEEK 5
OF
EASTER

[Jesus said,]
"I am the way, the truth, and the life;
no one goes to the Father except by me. . . .
Believe me when I say
that I am in the Father
and the Father is in me."

JOHN 14:6, 11

In 1965 huge areas of Canada and
the United States were blacked out
by the failure of an electric fuse
the size of a football.
All power to those huge areas
funneled through that single fuse.
Later, someone compared the fuse
to Jesus, saying,
"As that tiny fuse was the passageway
by which power went forth to
the United States and Canada,
so Jesus is the tiny passageway
by which we go forth to the Father."

To what extent is my own life and faith
reflected in this statement:
"When we have traveled all ways,
we shall come to the End of all ways,
who says 'I am the way'"?   SAINT ANDREW

Jesus is the way to the Father,
the truth about the Father,
and the life of the Father.

MONDAY
Easter
Week 5 _____

[Jesus said,]
"Whoever accepts my commandments
and obeys them
is the one who loves me.
My Father will love whoever loves me."

JOHN 14:21

One character in Richard Bach's
Jonathan Livingston Seagull
is Chiang, Jonathan's teacher.
When the day comes for Chiang
to say good-bye to his young student,
Jonathan knows it is a special moment.
He wonders what parting advice
his old teacher will give him.
Chiang utters it in just five words:
"Jonathan, keep working on love."
It is this same parting advice
that Jesus gave to his own disciples:
"Keep working on love."

If I asked Jesus how his parting advice
applied to me right now in my life,
how might he answer me?

We have learned
to fly in the air like birds
and to swim in the sea like fish.
But we have not learned
the simple act of living together.

MARTIN LUTHER KING, JR.

[In a final instruction to his disciples,
Jesus said,]
"Peace is what I leave with you;
it is my own peace that I give you."
JOHN 14:27

The great musician Pablo Casals
was also a tireless worker for peace.
When he announced plans
to circle the globe in a peace crusade,
he said:
"I am a man first, an artist second.
As a man,
my first obligation is to the welfare
of my fellowman.
I will endeavor to meet this obligation
through music–
the means God has given me–
since it transcends language,
politics and national boundaries.
My contribution to world peace
may be small.
But at least I will have given all I can."

Jesus said, "Happy are those
who work for peace" (MATTHEW 5:9).
What is one way I might work for peace?

World peace begins in each heart.
If the tree is to be green,
its individual leaves must be green.

WEDNESDAY
Easter
Week 5 _____

[Jesus said to his disciples,]
"You can do nothing without me.
Whoever does not remain in me
is thrown out like a branch and dries up."
JOHN 15:5–6

An old Jewish story concerns a woman
who stopped going to the synagogue.
One day the rabbi went to her house
and asked to sit with her by the fireplace.
For a long time, neither spoke.
Then the rabbi picked up a tongs,
took a glowing coal from the fireplace,
and set it on the hearth.
As the two watched,
the coal slowly lost its glow and died.
A few minutes later,
the old woman said, "I understand.
I'll come back to the synagogue."

Is there anything
that threatens to cut me off from Jesus
and cause me to lose my glow?
Is there anyone who has been cut off
from Jesus that I might help,
as the rabbi helped the old woman?

"We find comfort
among those who agree with us—
growth among those who don't."
FRANK A. CLARK

[Jesus said,]
"I love you just as the Father loves me;
remain in my love."

JOHN 15:9

A little girl was showing her dolls
to her granddmother.
Her grandmother asked her,
"Which one do you like most?"
The little girl said,
"Promise you won't laugh if I tell you."
Her grandmother promised.
Then the little girl picked up
the most miserable-looking doll of all.
"Why do you like that one most?"
asked her grandmother.
The little girl said, "Because it needs
my love more than the pretty ones do."

The little girl's love for the doll
reflects Jesus' love for us.
He loves us because we are sinners
and need his love most.
Jesus' love for us
and the girl's love for the tattered doll
invite me to ask: What is one way
that I can love more as they do?

No one needs love more
than someone who doesn't deserve it.

ANONYMOUS

FRIDAY
Easter
Week 5 _____

*[Jesus said,] "My commandment is this:
love one another, just as I love you."*
                                    JOHN 15:12

The British poet Leigh Hunt
wrote a poem called
"Abou ben Adhem."
One night Abou awoke and saw an angel
writing in a book the names
of those who loved God most.
Abou asked, "And is mine one?"
The angel replied, "Nay, not so."
Then Abou told the angel to write down
that he loved his fellowmen greatly.
The angel wrote and vanished.
"The next night / It came again
with a great awakening light, /
And showed the names
whom love of God had blessed, /
And lo! Ben Adhem's name
led all the rest."

If I asked the angel the same question
that Abou ben Adhem did,
how might the angel answer me?
How might I reply to the angel?

*"Whenever you did this
for one of the least important . . .
you did it for me!"*
                          MATTHEW 25:40

[Jesus said,]
"Remember what I told you:
'No slave is greater than his master.'
If they persecuted me,
they will persecute you too."

JOHN 15:20

An American warship was filled
with wounded prisoners of war.
The medical officer in charge
gave them such excellent care
that another officer complained, saying,
"Treat them the same way
that they treat our wounded."
The medical officer replied,
"I'm not going to play
by their set of rules, but by ours.
I'm going to do my best
to replace whatever hatred they have
in their hearts."

By what set of rules do I usually play:
those of Jesus,
or those of the world?
How comfortable am I in doing this?

He drew a circle that shut me out–
Heretic, rebel, a thing to flout.
But love and I had the wit to win.
We drew a circle that took him in.

EDWIN MARKHAM, *"Outwitted"*

WEEK 6
OF
EASTER

[Jesus said to his disciples,]
"Whoever accepts my commandments and
obeys them is the one who loves me. . . .
I too will love him
and reveal myself to him."

JOHN 14:21

An old legend tells
about an angel walking down the street,
carrying a torch in one hand
and a pail of water in the other.
"What are you going to do with those?"
someone asked. The angel replied,
"With the torch I'm going to burn down
the mansions of heaven;
and with the pail of water,
I'm going to put out the fires of hell.
Then we shall see who really loves God."
The angel's point is that many people
keep the commandments more out of
fear of punishment or hope of reward
than out of love for God.

What is the biggest reason
I keep the commandments:
fear of punishment,
hope of reward, or love of God?

The hand will not reach out for
what the heart does not long for.
GERMAN PROVERB

MONDAY
Easter
Week 6 _____

[Jesus said to his disciples,
"When the Holy Spirit comes,
you] will speak about me,
because you have been with me
from the very beginning."
                    JOHN 15:27

Former Penn State football star
D. J. Dozier knelt and prayed
after he scored in the Fiesta Bowl.
His action sparked instant criticism.
Coming to his defense, R. D. Lashar,
an outstanding high school kicker, said,
"Before and after each place kick,
I kneel and pray. The day someone tells me
I can't pray is the day I don't play!
It's a free country."
Sports fan Mark Roberts wrote,
"I find it refreshing to see someone
do something besides a silly dance . . .
and flaunting an oversized ego."

That I am called
to witness to Jesus is one thing.
How I witness to him is another.
What is probably the most convincing way
that I am witnessing to Jesus?

Every believer in this world
must become a spark of light.
                    POPE JOHN XXIII

[After telling his disciples
that he was going to the Father,
Jesus said,] "Now that I have told you,
your hearts are full of sadness.
But I am telling you the truth:
it is better for you that I go away,
because if I do not go,
the Helper [Spirit] will not come to you."

JOHN 16:6–7

In *The Ultimate Seduction,*
Charlotte Chandler quotes Israeli
Prime Minister Golda Meir as saying,
"I was never a beauty. There was a time
when I was sorry about that. . . .
It was only much later
that I realized that not being beautiful
was a blessing in disguise.
It forced me to develop
my inner resources."
What often begins as a cross in life
becomes a blessing.
What begins as sadness becomes a joy.

What is one thing about myself
that I found hard to accept at first
but from which I later benefitted much?

Defeat may serve as well as victory
to shake the soul and let the glory out.

EDWIN MARKHAM

WEDNESDAY
Easter
Week 6 _____

[Jesus said,]
"I have much more to tell you, but now
it would be too much for you to bear.
When, however, the Spirit comes,
who reveals the truth about God,
he will lead you into all the truth."
                              JOHN 16:12–13

While Kathryn Koob was a hostage in Iran,
angry mobs shouted outside her room,
almost around the clock.
One night she woke up with a start.
She says, "I turned quickly,
expecting to see one of my guards.
But no one was there."
Kathryn then adds that, for some reason,
she "was reminded of the Holy Spirit."
From then on,
the Spirit seemed to be with her in prison
in a special way.
She says, "He was teaching me love . . .
and new understanding."

In what area of my life, right now,
would I like the Holy Spirit to give me
new love and new understanding?

O Holy Spirit, Paraclete, perfect in us
the work begun by Jesus.
                              POPE JOHN XXIII

[Before ascending to the Father,
Jesus said to his disciples,]
"Go . . . to all peoples everywhere
and make them my disciples. . . .
And I will be with you always."
MATTHEW 28:19–20

A woman saw a little girl in the street
playing with filthy trash.
The child was poorly dressed
and ill-nourished.
The woman became angry and said to God,
"Why do you let a thing like that
happen in the world you created?
Why don't you do something about it?"
God replied, "I did do something about it;
I created you."

That story invites me to ask myself:
How seriously do I take Jesus' command
to transform our world into
the kind of place God created it to be?

The Ascension of Christ
is his liberation from all restrictions
of time and space.
It does not represent his removal
from earth,
but his constant presence everywhere
on earth.

WILLIAM TEMPLE

FRIDAY
Easter
Week 6 _____

[Jesus said,] "Now you are sad,
but I will see you again,
and your hearts will be filled with gladness,
the kind of gladness
that no one can take away from you."
                                    JOHN 16:22

A 13-year old girl was dead of leukemia.
While going through her belongings,
her parents found a poem
she had written during her illness.
It confirmed in a beautiful way
what Jesus says in today's gospel:
A portion of it reads:
"O God, I'm Free! . . .
Your hand came through the dark,
A faint spark; but it lit my soul.
My fire is burning, Lord.
No one can put it out.
O God, I'm Free!"
MISSION Magazine

The girl's poem invites me to pray,
O God, show me what I can do
to help your hand come through the dark
and light a spark in another's life.

Sometimes opportunity knocks,
but most of the time it sneaks up on you
and then quietly steals away.
                                    DOUG LARSEN

[Jesus said,]
"The Father will give you
whatever you ask of him in my name.
Until now you have not asked
for anything in my name;
ask and you will receive."

JOHN 16:23–24

Roland Stair tells this story.
A hospital chaplain learned that a patient
from his hometown was in Room 164.
But when the chaplain got to the room,
the expected patient was not there.
The chaplain apologized, saying,
"I probably made a mistake."
The patient in the room replied,
"It's no mistake, your being here;
I've been praying for the courage
to talk to you.
But I couldn't bring myself to do it.
And now you wander in here by mistake.
No, it was no mistake!"

What is one thing in my life that I would
like to do but lack the courage to do?
What is one thing I might do
to break through this situation?

Work as if everything depends on you.
Pray as if everything depends on God.
SAINT IGNATIUS OF LOYOLA

WEEK 7
OF
EASTER

[Jesus prayed to his Father,]
"Eternal life means
to know you, the only true God, and
to know Jesus Christ, whom you sent."
                                    JOHN 17:3

Mark Twain's wit and charm
made him popular not only in America
but also in Europe.
On one European trip, he was invited
to dine with a head of state.
When Twain's little daughter
learned of the invitation, she said,
"Daddy, you know every big person
there is to know, except God."
She was referring to the fact
that her daddy was not a religious man,
at least in the formal sense.

An example of Twain's irreligious wit
is this sentence from his *Notebook:*
"If Christ were here now,
there is one thing he would not be–
a Christian."
What is Twain's point
and to what extent might it be valid today?

Religion is not a way of looking
at certain things. It is a certain way
of looking at everything.
                                    ROBERT E. SEGAL

MONDAY
Easter
Week 7 _____

[Jesus said,]
"The time is coming . . .
when all of you will be scattered,
each one to his own home. . . .
The world will make you suffer.
But be brave!
I have defeated the world!"
                    JOHN 16:32–33

Jesus probably noticed the fear
on his disciples' faces when he told them
that they would have to suffer.
But their fear did not alarm Jesus.
He knew that fear is not a bad thing.
If used properly, it is a good thing.
Test pilot Chuck Yeager says:
"You feed off fear
as if it's a high-energy candy bar.
It keeps you focused and alert."
This is also the reasoning
behind Starbuck's comment
in *Moby Dick,* when he says
that the only men he wants in his boat
are men who are afraid of whales.

When was I really afraid in my life?
What do I fear most, right now?

Courage is being scared to death—
but saddling up anyway.
                    ACTOR JOHN WAYNE

Jesus . . . looked up to heaven
and said,
"Father, the hour has come. . . .
I have finished the work
you gave me to do. . . .
I have made you known
to those you gave me."
JOHN 17:1, 4, 6

This picture of Jesus at prayer recalls
an episode from Dorothy Day's life.
She says that before her conversion
and her work among New York's poor,
she often spent the night in taverns.
Then, on her way home,
around six o'clock in the morning,
she would stop in at St. Joseph's Church
on Sixth Avenue.
What attracted her to St. Joseph's
was the sight of the people praying
at early Mass. She writes:
"I longed for their faith. . . .
So I used to go in and kneel in the back."

Can I recall a time when I was moved
by the faith of people at prayer?

If you Christians in India, in Britain,
or in America were like your Bible,
you would conquer India in five years.
INDIAN BRAHMAN TO A MISSIONARY

WEDNESDAY
Easter
Week 7 _____

[Jesus prayed for his disciples, saying,]
"Holy Father! . . .
I gave them your message. . . .
I sent them into the world,
just as you sent me into the world.
And for their sake I dedicate myself to you,
in order that they, too,
may be truly dedicated to you."
JOHN 17:11, 14, 18–19

Legend says that when Jesus returned
to heaven, the angel Gabriel asked him
if all people knew of his love for them.
"Oh, no!" said Jesus, "only a handful do."
Gabriel was shocked and asked,
"How will the rest learn?"
Jesus said, "The *handful* will tell them."
"But," said Gabriel,
"What if they let you down?
What if they meet opposition?
What if they become discouraged?
Don't you have a back-up plan?"
"No," said Jesus, "I'm counting on them
not to let me down."

What convinces me
that Jesus' followers won't let him down?

I used to ask God to help me.
Then I asked if I might help him.
HUDSON TAYLOR

[Jesus spoke to his Father
about his disciples in these words:]
"I pray not only for them,
but also for those who believe in me
because of their message.
I pray that they may all be one."
JOHN 17:20-21

Nobel Prize winner Alexis Carrel writes:
"When we pray we link ourselves
to the inexhaustible motive power
which spins the universe.
We ask that a part of this power
be apportioned to our needs.
Even in asking,
our deficiencies are filled and
we rise strengthened and refreshed. . . .
True prayer is a way of life.
The truest life is literally
a life of prayer."

What is one way that prayer
has had an effect on my life
since I began praying regularly?

Prayer is like the turning on
of an electric switch.
It does not create the current;
it simply provides a channel
through which the current can flow.
MAX HANDEL

FRIDAY
Easter
Week 7 _____

[Three times Jesus asked Simon Peter,]
"Simon son of John, do you love me?"
[Three times Peter responded,]
"Yes, Lord . . .
you know that I love you."
[Three times Jesus commissioned Peter,
saying,] "Take care of my sheep."
JOHN 21:16

Peter's triple affirmation of love
erased his triple denial of Jesus,
which he uttered the night before Jesus
was crucified (MARK 14:72).
And Jesus' triple response to Peter
commissioned Peter to succeed him
as shepherd of the flock
of his followers on earth.

What is my attitude toward the shepherds
of God's flock on earth today?
What one thing, especially, helps me
to see beyond their human weaknesses
to the commission Jesus gave them?

[The Church] is a society of sinners.
It is the only society in the world
in which membership
is based upon a single qualification,
that the candidate be unworthy
of membership.
CHARLES CLAYTON MORRISON

Now, there are many other things
that Jesus did.
If they were all written down one by one,
I suppose that the whole world
could not hold the books
that would be written.

JOHN 21:25

A pickup truck pulled off the road.
A voice from the cab yelled to
a bunch of Boy Scouts in the back:
"Prayer time. Finish your rosaries
while I finish my office."
(The office is a book of daily prayer
made up mainly of scripture readings.)
Father Joyce sat next to the headlight
and began praying his office.
Almost immediately, a rig rolled up
and the driver said, "Need any help?"
"No," said Father Joyce, "just reading!"
As the rig rolled off, the priest smiled
at the trucker's parting words:
"Must be a darn good book!"

What story/passage in the "good book"
speaks to me in a special way? Why?

I know the Bible is inspired
because it finds me at a greater depth
of my being than any other book.
SAMUEL TAYLOR COLERIDGE

PENTECOST

SUNDAY

Pentecost _____

*[Jesus breathed on his disciples
and said,] "Receive the Holy Spirit."*
JOHN 20:22

The Cross and the Switchblade
describes Rev. David Wilkerson's work
with young derelicts in New York City.
One firsthand report in the book
comes from a heroin user named Joe.
He says: "The Holy Spirit
is called the Comforter, they told me.
When I thought of comfort, I thought of
a bottle of wine and a dozen goof balls.
But these guys
were talking about comfort from heaven
where I could feel clean later.
I got to wanting this. . . .
I cried to God for help and that's when
he [the Holy Spirit] came. . . .
I didn't want any more drugs.
I loved everybody. For the first time
in my life I felt clean."

What role does the Holy Spirit play
in my life?
Do I pray to the Holy Spirit?

*O come, O Holy Spirit, come!
Come as holy light and lead us.
Come as holy truth and teach us.*
ANCIENT PRAYER (adapted)

Weekly Meeting Format

CALL TO PRAYER

> *The leader begins each weekly meeting*
> *by having someone light a candle*
> *and then three people pray the following:*

FIRST READER:

Jesus said,
"I am the light of the world. . . .
Whoever follows me
will have the light of life
and will never walk in darkness."

JOHN 8:12

SECOND READER:

Lord Jesus, you also said
that where two or three
come together in your name,
you are there with them.
The light of this candle
symbolizes your presence among us.

THIRD READER:

And, Lord Jesus,
where you are,
there, too,
are the Father and the Holy Spirit.
So we begin our meeting
in the presence and the name
of the Father,
the Son,
and the Holy Spirit.